# HAL•LEONARD
## INSTRUMENTAL PLAY-ALONG

AUDIO ACCESS INCLUDED

**PLAYBACK+**
Speed • Pitch • Balance • Loop

# CLASSIC POP SONGS

## CLARINET

T0086647

Audio arrangements by Peter Deneff

To access audio visit:
**www.halleonard.com/mylibrary**
Enter Code
5866-6903-1830-5253

ISBN 978-1-5400-0244-0

## HAL•LEONARD®

7777 W. BLUEMOUND RD. P.O. BOX 13819 MILWAUKEE, WI 53213

Visit Hal Leonard Online at
**www.halleonard.com**

# BRIDGE OVER TROUBLED WATER

Clarinet

Words and Music by
PAUL SIMON

# CANDLE IN THE WIND

Clarinet

Words and Music by ELTON JOHN
and BERNIE TAUPIN

# DUST IN THE WIND

Clarinet

Words and Music by
KERRY LIVGREN

# EVERY BREATH YOU TAKE

CLARINET

Music and Lyrics by
STING

# FIRE AND RAIN

CLARINET

Words and Music by
JAMES TAYLOR

# HAVE I TOLD YOU LATELY

CLARINET

Words and Music by
VAN MORRISON

# GOOD VIBRATIONS

CLARINET

Words and Music by BRIAN WILSON
and MIKE LOVE

11

# HEAVEN

CLARINET

Words and Music by BRYAN ADAMS
and JIM VALLANCE

# LEAN ON ME

CLARINET

Words and Music by
BILL WITHERS

# SHE'S ALWAYS A WOMAN

Clarinet

Words and Music by
BILLY JOEL

# WITH A LITTLE HELP FROM MY FRIENDS

Clarinet

Words and Music by JOHN LENNON
and PAUL McCARTNEY

# TEARS IN HEAVEN

Clarinet

Words and Music by ERIC CLAPTON
and WILL JENNINGS